The Smart Habit Guide

37 Small Life Changes Your Brain Will Thank You for Making

By I. C. Robledo

www.Amazon.com/author/icrobledo

The Smart Habit Guide: 37 Small Life Changes Your Brain Will Thank You for Making

Disclaimer

Table of Contents

Introduction

I have sometimes heard people refer to each other as smart or dumb, as if you had to be one or the other. I've noticed that very smart people tend to implement what I would call 'smart habits' into their lives. And people who aren't viewed as being smart often do not. With smart habits, anyone can work on improving their intellectual abilities. I believe that most of the time, people who don't see themselves as smart just haven't learned about the right habits to make better use of their minds. Whether you see yourself as smart or not, this book can help you on the path to developing your intellect. This is possible through the power of smart habits.

I. C. Robledo

What is a Smart Habit?

A smart habit is just an action you perform regularly because it helps to further develop your mind and intellect. This entire book will be about smart habits and how you can use them in your life.

Why Smart Habits Matter

I went through many years when I was younger thinking that I was dumb and slow. This wasn't actually true, I just hadn't realized that to develop a smart mind, you have to adopt habits that are challenging and push your mind to work. School can teach you some things, but they usually won't teach you about which habits will help you in your intellectual development. When learning begins and ends in the classroom, you're a lot less likely to meet your potential.

The secret about smart people is that they weren't born that way. It takes some work to cultivate a great mind. But imagine someone who spends all of his time watching reruns of sitcoms. How smart could such a person be if there wasn't any focus on doing something challenging? It's a myth that smart people have it easy. They often work hard, perhaps daily, to further their minds. They're familiar with smart habits, and they practice using them regularly.

Allow me to tell you a bit about my background before we go further into what smart habits are all about. Back in high school I was a B student taking some of the tougher courses offered. I had a friend who struggled to get Cs and who took easier classes, and he always had this idea that I was so much smarter than him. He believed that I couldn't possibly understand how tough he had it because everything just came easy for me. He must have thought I was born to be smart and that was the end of it. But he was wrong. If I never worked on adopting smart habits, I wouldn't be smart at all.

One time this friend told me he was failing geometry. I offered to help him since I knew geometry pretty well. He rejected my offer, and it seemed to me that he had given up on himself. I reminded him several times that I was willing to help for no cost, but he never took me up on it. I thought about this situation for a while, and I realized that this friend of mine was not dumb, even though he did end up failing his class. He just didn't realize that smart people have certain habits that give them advantages. They perform better because they're good at using habits that work for them. One of those habits, as it turns out, is being willing to get help when you really need it (Habit #30).

I first discovered the power of smart habits through observing my parents. They were both immigrants to the US and they worked very hard to build good careers for themselves. When I was younger, I noticed my mother would ask many detailed questions pretty regularly. If we were at the doctor's office and I was sick, she'd make sure she knew what to do in any possible circumstance. She'd ask about side effects, about if I had a problem that could get worse, and so forth. I used to think asking so many questions was a sign of having little understanding of something. But I later came to understand that asking many questions is exactly how people come to truly understand a topic. It was a smart habit (Habit #6).

I also learned from my father. He was often well informed on events around the world. He would read newspapers, science magazines, and books of various topics. He would talk about history, politics, science, and many other areas as well. As a child I would sometimes struggle to understand as he went into detailed explanations as to why the world is the way it is. An important point I did understand from observing my father was that you can learn quite a bit through reading. That is a smart habit as well (Habit #1).

I've been interested in how smart people do well in life since I was in high school. Back then, as I said, I didn't feel very smart. I feared growing up to be unintelligent and slow, and surrounded by highly intelligent people who would laugh at my stupidity. This scenario sounds silly, but that was my fear in high school.

My way of dealing with this worry of being intellectually inferior was to pay close attention to the things smart people did. It didn't take me long to notice that they used specific habits. If I ever notice someone do something intellectually impressive, I would often ask exactly how they did it. Simply by asking questions I've gotten a better understanding of how smart people think, work, and what kind of habits they use.

As I've gotten older I've amassed a list of such habits. This book is a compilation of the most useful smart habits I know, and it includes examples of how I've used them or how I've seen them put to good use. Before we get to the habits themselves, I want to share some information that will help you get the best use from this book.

Five Realizations to Maximize the Benefits of Smart Habits

Realization #1: You can increase your abilities if you work at it.

Dr. Carol Dweck, author of "Mindset: the New Psychology of Success", has done research into people who hold different points of view on intelligence. She discusses people with 'fixed' and 'growth' mindsets. The people with a fixed mindset think that we have the abilities we are born with, and there isn't much we can do about changing that. The people with a growth mindset think if we work hard at something then we can always improve our abilities and get better. People who have a growth mindset tend to work harder on tough problems and perform better, and those with a fixed mindset tend to give up on problems they think are beyond them. To boil this down, if you think you can get smarter and improve your abilities, then you can. If you think you can't, then you'll make things much harder on yourself.

Realization #2: The habits we adopt are important to how smart we can become.

Thinking smarter is important, but our actions are just as important if not more so. It's important that we learn the habits that allow us to improve our mental abilities, our learning, and our performance. This is what I was talking about above. My high school friend thought I was so much smarter than him, but he didn't realize I had to study a lot and spend much of my time struggling to understand. It didn't just come to me automatically. I'm sure the fact that I studied hard until I understood something was more important to my grades than any sort of natural ability.

Realization #3: Smart habits are unlike other habits.

Here is a trick you should learn. There is no one habit that will solve all of your problems. But if there was only one super-habit you learned, it should be what I'm about to tell you here. Smart habits should be challenging to you in some way. They should present a kind of struggle. They should present something new. If your habit no longer does this, it's time to find a new one. However, if you find a task to be new and challenging, then it's a smart habit you can adopt. When you master a habit, this is a good time to add a new habit into your life because you are now ready for a bigger challenge.

Realization #4: You need to have knowledge to gain knowledge.

All new knowledge is built up on prior things you've learned. Be willing to learn the basics of something before you progress to more advanced topics. Get used to checking out dictionary definitions and Wikipedia entries of something completely new before you decide to tackle the topic in a more in depth way. By learning in this manner you'll avoid frustration and the feeling of wanting to quit.

Realization #5: Getting smart is a lifestyle choice.

You either choose to regularly implement smart habits into your life, or you choose not to. Some people may naturally tend to understand things a little more quickly or slowly than others, but what is under your control is the habits and actions you choose to do. The lifestyle involves doing multiple smart things, not just one. It involves a positive enthusiastic attitude toward challenge, and not one of wanting to quit at the first sign of a problem.

I've presented these realizations to you because if you have them, you'll be able to make better progress in your pursuits. If you don't have them, you can become your own greatest obstacle toward becoming a smarter individual.

Advantages to Using Smart Habits

Implementing smart habits gives you advantages in work and in life. I've noticed some of these in myself when I've adopted a new habit, and I've noticed them in other smart people as well. You've probably seen this for yourself at some point too.

These are some of the advantages of people who adopt smart habits:

- Learning and doing new things becomes easier
- Faster thinking and comprehension
- Better preparedness at work
- Seeing patterns more quickly
- Remembering things more easily and clearly

Why is this? Truly smart people are in the habit of routinely exercising their minds. They won't go a day without challenging themselves in some way. The brain is a complex and special organ. The most important thing you should know about the brain is that it responds to challenge. This is why some people say the brain is like a muscle. Obviously the brain is not a muscle, but the more you exercise and challenge it, the more you will learn, understand, and remember.

Implementing Smart Habits in Your Life

I originally thought I might recommend certain time guidelines for the smart habits in this book, but I decided not to. These habits are meant to be simple and effective so anyone can apply them to see improvements in their life. Even though I've chosen such habits, there is no one time per habit that will work for everyone. One person may spend five minutes performing a habit, and another person may take an hour or more. I will leave that choice up to you, depending on what you wish to achieve. Of course, you should realize that the more time and effort you invest, the more likely you are to receive benefits from implementing the smart habits in this book.

Before You Continue...

As a thank you for reading, I want you to have a free guide called:

Step Up Your Learning: Free Tools to Learn Almost Anything

Have you ever wondered what the best sites and resources for learning are? It takes time and effort to figure out which sites are worth it and which are not. I hope to save you some of that time so you can spend more of it learning instead of searching the Internet.

In the past ten years or so, there has been a free learning revolution happening. More and more resources for learning are becoming available to the public at no cost. With so many new ones coming out, it's easy to miss out on some of the great learning opportunities available. Fortunately for you, this guide is short at around 4,000 words, and tells you exactly what you need to know.

The guide stems from my own experiences of using a variety of learning sites and resources. In it, you will discover the best places to go for learning at no cost. Also, I'll explain which resources are best for you, depending on your learning goals.

<u>You can download this free guide as a PDF by typing this website into your browser:</u>

http://bit.ly/Robledo

Now, let's get back on topic.

Learn Something Every Day

It's a good idea to learn something new regularly. The smartest most informed people I know tend to listen to NPR (National Public Radio), read frequently, and they always seem to be aware of current events or something new happening. They don't allow themselves to stagnate in their knowledge and abilities. It's not necessary to make this too complicated. You don't need to solve a math problem that's puzzled mathematicians for centuries. You could simply learn one little thing every day. In time, your knowledge will add up and you'll be much better informed.

#1. Read Books, Articles, and Stories

Through reading you can learn about pretty much anything. If you can think about something, a book has probably been written on the topic.

Luckily there is a great abundance of material to read. There are millions of books in existence, and countless articles being published all of the time. You can choose from newspapers, blogs, magazines, books and eBooks. Some reading material can be paid for, but libraries and online resources are good for finding free items as well.

Although reading is a great habit, I've found that some people get too caught up in counting how many books or articles they read. They aim to read more and more, rather than to truly think about and understand what they read. I find that it's important to take some time to build connections and get a deeper understanding of what I read. Along with this, it's important to choose good reading material to begin with. Obviously, not every book is a good source of information or good for intellectual development. Both fiction and nonfiction titles can be great to read, it just depends what you want to gain from the experience.

Reading, although quite obviously a smart habit, is one of my favorite habits. I may read over twenty or thirty books, and hundreds of news and blog articles in the course of a year. This makes me somewhat conversational in a variety of fields, or at least to the point where I can more quickly pick up new things.

How to apply this habit

- Read a newspaper such as your local paper, The Week, BBC, or the Economist
- Read a niche blog post
- Read a Wikipedia page you're curious about, or a random Wikipedia article
- Read fictional short stories
- Browse free books
- Browse Open Culture's big list of free eBooks
- Browse Open Culture's big list of free Textbooks

Websites & Resources

- http://theweek.com
- http://www.bbc.com
- http://www.economist.com
- http://en.wikipedia.org/wiki/special:random
- http://www.world-english.org/stories.htm
- http://www.freebooks.com
- http://www.openculture.com/free_ebooks
- http://www.openculture.com/free_textbooks

#2. Watch Informative Video Programs

By watching informative videos, you can get a much more vivid picture of the things you may read about. You can read a great description of what the Sistine chapel is like, or what the Panama Canal is like, but seeing an actual video about these places will really give you a more accurate picture. It will help a place come to life in your mind. Of course, if you have the option to travel, then this is definitely worth considering.

Like with reading, you can learn about quite a range of topics through video. In fact, it's easier than ever to look up a video of anything on YouTube and find it in seconds. Videos can be especially useful for learning how to do specific things that are visual. For example, it probably makes more sense to learn Yoga or how to tie a tie through watching someone do it than to read a manual.

Personally, some of my favorite videos to watch are TED talks. TED stands for technology, entertainment, design. They cover a very wide range of topics such as new technology, aquatic life, music, and a whole lot more. TED talks are a great starting point for learning about many different topics. Their videos often inspire me to think in new directions and motivate me to learn more about something on my own.

How to apply this habit

- Watch National Geographic videos – short videos under 5 minutes long

- Watch TED talks – most are around 10-20 minutes long

- Watch documentaries – there are short to full length videos

- Watch NOVA (PBS) videos – 50 minute episodes as well as 5 minute clips

- Use Google Video or YouTube to search for anything you want to learn – of course, you have to judge for yourself if the source is a good one since people can post anything

- Browse through OpenCulture's great list of free movies and videos

Websites & Resources

- http://video.nationalgeographic.com/
- http://www.ted.com/
- http://www.reddit.com/r/Documentaries/
- http://video.pbs.org/program/nova/
- http://www.google.com/videohp?hl=en
- https://www.youtube.com/
- http://www.openculture.com/ freemoviesonline

#3. Listen to Informative Podcasts

Listening to podcasts (online radio episodes) is a useful habit to have because it presents another way to learn and absorb new information. You may prefer to get your information through reading, viewing, or just listening, but the most important thing is to make a continuous effort to learn.

The easiest way to listen to the podcasts you like is to subscribe to them so you know when a new show is released. You can find many podcasts online, but one of the greatest repositories of them will be through iTunes. Another easy way to get started fast is to try the Podcasts app or the iTunes U app if you have an iPhone or iPad.

Some people love listening to podcasts all of the time. I usually prefer reading or watching videos, but if those options aren't available or if I want to try something different, podcasts can be great. It's a good idea to be familiar with some informative podcasts so you can listen to them when you have time. Podcast episodes are especially convenient because you can play them and pause them as you like.

Podcasts haven't been around as long as reading or video, but they've come a long way. You should be able to find podcasts on almost any topic at this point. It's good to realize that most podcasts can last around a half hour or more per show, but there are also shorter ones that are quite good as well.

Sometimes when it's nice out I like to go for a walk and listen to a podcast. It's good to get some exercise, enjoy the outdoors, and learn something new all at once. If you're going to start listening to podcasts, I'd recommend keeping earphones with you in public to avoid disturbing anyone.

How to apply this habit

- Download iTunes for the greatest access to podcasts – you can also download the Podcasts app or the iTunes U app on your iPad or iPhone

- Subscribe to an NPR podcast like "NPR topics: story of the day" (available on iTunes or Podcasts app)

- Subscribe to Ted Talks (available on iTunes or Podcasts app)

- Subscribe to courses and lectures (available on iTunes U app on iPad and iPhone)

- Use the search feature (on iTunes or the Podcasts app) to learn about something that interest you

Websites & Resources

- http://www.apple.com/itunes/download

#4. Look up New Words

When you learn a new word, it becomes easier to understand what you read. Imagine reading a document where every third word is a new one you've never seen before. It would almost be like reading something in a different language. You'd probably be very confused and have little idea what the content is really about. When you take some time to expand your vocabulary, you will be much less likely to be completely confused, no matter what you read. The best thing to do is to develop your vocabulary gradually. As you might guess, there is generally a strong relationship between someone's vocabulary and their IQ.

Sometimes learning a new word can be a powerful experience. If you look at an unabridged dictionary entry, there may be an image representation of the word. There may be a pronunciation key to show you exactly how to say the word. You will probably also see the language of origin displayed. There are also likely to be multiple meanings to the word. If you learn all of these details about words, you'll learn a great deal about all sorts of things. Words are our way of representing everything. It only makes sense that the more words you know, the better understanding you'll have of more and more concepts.

With learning about words, you'll be able to understand complex topics more easily. For example, if you enter into a discussion among college professors, it may at first seem intimidating. But if you knew the dictionary definition of a few key words used in the discussion, such as multilateral, gregarious, and, patrician, perhaps the conversation wouldn't seem quite as difficult. All of a sudden, the conversation would turn from difficult to follow into something that actually is quite simple to understand. Even learning a few key words can add great power to your ability to understand.

I've had a habit for learning new words since I was fairly young. I was the youngest in my home, and most of the friends and relatives I spent time with were older than me when I was a child. I learned that it made me uncomfortable to feel lost when new words were used, and the best way to tackle that problem was to look them up. At this point, I've found it's worth it to try to figure out the meaning of a word from context. If I can't figure out what it means or I'm still not sure, I'll look it up. By practicing your ability to learn words in context, you'll improve, and even if you aren't completely sure of what a word means, most of the time you'll have a good idea. I don't look up every new word I hear, but if I've heard it or seen it multiple times I usually will.

How to apply this habit

- When you read or hear a word you don't know, try to figure out the meaning from context – If you're still not sure, look up the meaning and write it down

- Use a new word you learned in a sentence, or in a conversation so you're more likely to remember it

- Subscribe to receive a Merriam-Webster word of the day in your email

- Read Merriam-Webster's Vocabulary Builder – a guide with excellent words worth knowing that also includes word origins and commonly used word roots that usually originate from Latin or Greek

Websites & Resources

- http://www.merriam-webster.com/word-of-the-day

- http://www.amazon.com/dp/B003IS768K

#5. Learn and Practice Speaking a New Language

Studies have supported that knowing more than one language is helpful for high level thought, multi-tasking, and sustained attention. Bilingual people need to switch between thinking about two languages often, and doing so strengthens their ability to switch between different tasks even if unrelated to language. Another important finding is that being bilingual is good for maintaining cognitive function. For example, the onset of dementia symptoms is delayed by up to five years in bilingual patients.

Learning a new language is a great challenge for your mind and your memory. I don't want you to underestimate the challenge and time commitment of truly learning a new language. This isn't something you'll be able to pull off in a weekend. If you want to learn in your spare time as you have 15 free minutes here and there, that may be doable, but the learning will be very gradual.

A nice benefit of learning a new language is that it's a great opportunity to learn about other cultures. Different languages use words in unique ways. Sometimes there is no direct translation for a concept, so the best way to understand a foreign concept is to learn the traditions and culture and language that go with it. If you are learning Spanish for example, you may find it interesting when you learn about specific dishes that are native to many Spanish speaking countries. If you're curious enough, you may try making them on your own. In this scenario, learning a new language could lead to learning new recipes and food. This in turn may involve learning names that don't have a direct translation in your native language.

In my experience, the most useful way to learn a language is to practice it. Of course, everyone needs to learn basic vocabulary and get a good idea of how the words go together, but after that it's important to practice speaking. At the very least, practice pronouncing words correctly. If you can, immerse yourself in a language if you want to learn it. The most dramatic way to do this is to live in a foreign country, but that isn't necessary. You can visit foreign language speaking forums online, make a friend on skype who is native to another country, find a pen pal, or host a student from another country. With something like language learning, it can also be a big help to have a friend who wants to learn with you. This way you can keep each other motivated and practice with each other.

Another thing to consider is that there are more languages than the traditional ones we think of. Don't forget about Esperanto – the most widely spoken constructed language in the world, or sign language which is clearly useful for communicating with deaf persons. You might also consider learning

Morse code, although it isn't strictly a language, it's a way to transform language into a different format of dots and dashes.

How to apply this habit

- Use Duolingo (available on the Web, iOS, Android and Windows Phone 8.1) to learn the basics of a language

- Visit r/languagelearning to join a community of language learners

- Practice speaking with a native speaker

- Watch a movie in the language you are studying (with subtitles if desired)

- Read children's books in the language you want to learn

- Browse through Open Culture's big list of sites to learn 48 languages

- Read some helpful language learning articles:

  o I Learned to Speak Four Languages in a Few Years: Here's How by Gabriel Wyner

  o 12 Rules for Learning Foreign Languages in Record Time by Tim Ferriss

Websites & Resources

- https://www.duolingo.com/
- http://www.reddit.com/r/languagelearning/
- http://www.openculture.com/freelanguagelessons
- http://lifehacker.com/5903288/i-learned-to-speak-four-languages-in-a-few-years-heres-how
- http://fourhourworkweek.com/2014/03/21/how-to-learn-a-foreign-language-2

#6. Ask Questions

Many people are afraid to ask questions for fear of appearing to not be all that smart. However, curiosity and questions are a great driver of intelligence. When you don't know something it's important to ask questions because it is a great opportunity to learn something new. In school with a room full of students, questions can be looked at as an unwanted distraction, but it is unfair to think of questions in that way. I still remember a few good teachers I had who would remind the class that if anyone has a question then they should ask it. This is because it was pretty likely that at least one other student would have the same question in mind but be worried about asking and appearing foolish.

Even if you are in a situation where you realize that you don't know something basic that most people seem to know, it's important to ask questions. There is so much to know in this world that no one will know it all. We're all allowed to be ignorant of some things, as long as we recognize that ignorance and try to begin the path toward understanding. It's important to realize that before someone can progress to a complex and advanced level of understanding, first a basic understanding must be met.

When I ask questions, I find that I'm much more active in how I pay attention to the responses. Often times I'll ask a question, the expert or the knowledgeable person I'm talking to responds, then I'll ask another. The cycle repeats. Often, the answer to my question just makes me realize something else I don't know. One of the most rewarding things is to find someone informed and wise who is more than willing to answer a variety of questions.

How to apply this habit

- Ask questions at work or in meetings and try to understand *how* things work and *why* they work that way, rather than just knowing *what* needs to be done

- Practice questioning assumptions that you make every day – and consider alternative viewpoints to the ones you hold

- E-mail an expert on the internet with a specific question

- Use forums/communities like Quora, Reddit, or Stack Exchange to ask a question to people with similar interests as you

Websites & Resources

- https://www.quora.com
- http://www.reddit.com
- http://stackexchange.com

#7. Investigate Concepts More Deeply

The world is more rich and full of detail than we may ever realize. If you make yourself learn about those details, you will perceive the world more accurately. This is what it means to be highly intelligent. You see things closer to how they actually are. Instead of something just being a piece of wood, it's oak or maple. Instead of just skin, it's the epidermis (i.e., outer layer of skin). By learning such details, you'll be much better prepared to use the information you gain in the real world. The point of this habit is to delve deeper into the things that we learn, rather than being satisfied with just knowing the basics.

Knowing the names of things helps you categorize them better. As children we quickly learn big classification schemes. We learn what kinds of creatures are animals, what kinds are bugs, and what kinds of things we refer to as trees. As we get older, many of us settle for some of these broad categories and don't continue to learn more deeply about them. Many of us may see the world actually not much differently than children. If we choose to learn more deeply then we will gain a thorough understanding of the topics we feel are important.

When I was around seventeen years old, my grandfather's wife asked me a question. You should realize that she had never had the opportunity to go to high school. In her hand was an insect and she asked me if I knew what it was. I'm sure she expected me to know. I was finishing high school and I was getting decent grades. Soon I would be headed to college, to bigger ambitions and opportunities. But going back to the insect in her hand, I actually had no idea what it was. It might have been common to the area, but I had never paid any attention to it. This made me realize how little we sometimes know even about the things right in front of us. Smart people take some time to learn about the things that are right under their noses.

How to apply this habit

- For any object, ask yourself what it's made up of, what type of thing is it, or how to classify it more deeply – you can then do an online search or browse an encyclopedia to help you answer these questions

- Identify specific insects, trees, or birds you see

- Using a search engine, type in ["Identify" + Type of thing you want to identify]

Websites & Resources

- http://www.insectidentification.org/identifying.asp

- http://www.arborday.org/trees/whatTree

- http://animals.nationalgeographic.com/animals/birding/backyard-bird-identifier

#8. Enroll in an Online Course

The world of education has been changing over the past several years. We now have access to all kinds of high quality education online for free. MIT launched an open courseware program back in 2002. Since then, many other universities have joined as well, through programs such as Coursera and EdX, all aiming to make education more accessible to the public. Educational programs like these are referred to as MOOCs (Massive Open Online Courses). Most if not all of these courses are offered at no cost.

While the certificates or even degrees offered by such online programs may not lead directly to jobs, you can still learn from leading professors and experts and often have access to forums with other eager to learn students.

A great thing about these courses is you can find them in a variety of fields, such as mathematics, music, sociology, computer software, biology, and plenty of others. The courses are typically taught in a lecture format with PowerPoint slides or some other kind of notes available. Some courses take more time and effort, and others may be more leisurely.

MOOCs like Coursera and EdX can be great for people who have enjoyed the college experience or for people who would like to go to college but who don't have the means to do so. It's good for people who like to listen, who want a community (in the form of a forum with students and a professor), and who don't mind being assigned some homework to make sure that they understand the material. Of course, attendance and homework is optional, but you wouldn't get the most out of these courses unless you do these things.

There is another site that isn't formally a MOOC, but still quite useful. It's called Khan Academy and I often prefer this site because Salman Khan, the founder, is an especially engaging teacher. Although he isn't a professor, he has Bachelor's degrees from MIT in mathematics, electrical engineering, and computer science. From MIT he also holds Master's degrees in electrical engineering and computer science, and he has a Master's of Business Administration from Harvard. Clearly, he's very well educated and he has a passion for learning and teaching. Even if not a MOOC, Khan Academy is an excellent learning resource.

I would encourage you to try both MOOCs and Khan Academy and see what you think, but I tend to prefer Khan Academy because it offers very short, clear, and engaging introductions to all kinds of topics. I've learned about biology and world history on the site in some of my free time. However, if you'd like to learn very deeply and to an advanced level, you may prefer to enroll in a MOOC instead.

How to apply this habit

- Watch videos and participate at Khan Academy

- Sign up for a class through the Open Education Consortium

- Sign up for a class on MIT OpenCourseWare, Coursera or EdX

- Browse through Open Culture's massive collection of MOOCs

- Browse through Open Culture's massive collection of online courses from top universities

Websites & Resources

- https://www.khanacademy.org

- http://www.oeconsortium.org/courses

- http://ocw.mit.edu/index.htm

- https://www.coursera.org

- https://www.edx.org

- http://www.openculture.com/free_certificate_courses

- http://www.openculture.com/freeonlinecourses

#9. Engage in Online Social Learning

There are plenty of great communities online where you can learn about niche topics. Reddit, Quora, and Stack Exchange are good places to start. However, there are countless numbers of forums and online groups where people meet up to talk about their favorite topics.

The great thing about these social communities is that they often provide a wealth of valuable information. These groups are very interested in their particular topics, so they often stay up to date on the newest things happening. They're also a great source of feedback. If you have questions, issues, or if there is something you have trouble understanding, one of these forums is likely to be very helpful to you.

Many of these sites have a lot of useful material to read. You might find a great introduction to your topic of interest. You also may find people or material that can point you to the best resources for your particular situation or your level of knowledge in your topic.

For some people who get bored with dry material, or who really enjoy socializing, this sort of learning could be a great fit. It combines socializing and learning. You can learn, teach, and practice what you learn with a community of people interested in the same things. It can be a lot of fun to try out the advice of forum members and come back to let them know how your progress is going or if you ran into any new problems. By doing this, you'll be involved in a community that helps each other learn and grow in expertise together.

How to apply this habit

- Visit Reddit and consider joining subreddits like r/answers (ask questions about anything), r/askscience (ask questions to scientists and experts), r/changemyview (learn different perspectives on hot issues), and r/iwanttolearn (get advice on how to learn anything), and anything else of interest

- Visit Quora or Stack Exchange and engage in the topics you're interested in

- Go to Google and search [Niche you are interested in + "forum"]

Websites & Resources

- http://www.reddit.com/r/answers
- http://www.reddit.com/r/askscience
- http://www.reddit.com/r/changemyview
- http://www.reddit.com/r/IWantToLearn
- https://www.quora.com
- http://stackexchange.com

#10. Learn within Your Community

Another option besides learning online is to learn through some kind of a local group or class if you have the time. A lot of the examples in this book so far have been about ways to learn online, and this is because I often find it easier to learn flexibly around whatever my schedule happens to be. Of course, when you choose a learning opportunity in real life, there tends to be less flexibility, as you must show up at a certain meeting time to be included. Also, online learning is often free, whereas real life courses usually aren't.

Even though learning online may be easier and cheaper, there are a lot of benefits to getting involved in learning and activities in real life, so this is an important outlet to consider. Some of those benefits are figuring out how things work under natural conditions and making connections with people.

In many places there are local classes or groups that meet up to learn more deeply about a topic, or to practice a specific skill. If you live in a moderate to big sized city, there will likely be some kind of opportunities that you can get involved with. Of course, the smaller of an area you live in, the more difficult it may be to find local learning opportunities.

How to apply this habit

- Read local newspapers to find out about upcoming gatherings and events in your area

- Check community bulletin boards at places like the local library for events and group meetings

- Go to Meetup.com and look for groups interested in the same things as you – these are groups that meet in real life and are searchable by city

- Google ["Learn" + topic of interest + city and state] to find local learning opportunities in your interest area

  ○ Topics you might you may consider searching are book clubs, self-defense classes, art and pottery classes, swimming classes, dance classes, board game enthusiast groups, or card game groups

Websites & Resources

Http://www.meetup.com

Challenge Yourself and Try New Things

The greater the challenges you expose yourself to, the more meaningful your learning will be. One of the most important parts of being a smart individual is searching for challenges and welcoming them. A key reason smart people are smart is because they don't back down easily from an intellectual challenge. They persist with intellectual challenges until they fully understand the problem or topic. It's a great mental exercise to make yourself think in depth about something or to try something completely new that you're not at all familiar with.

#11. Play Games that Involve Critical Thinking, Planning, or Calculating

Playing games challenges your mind with problems and makes you look for solutions. The only part that matters in how you choose a game is that it should provide a challenge of some kind. If you've played a game so many times that you can practically win it in your sleep, it's a good time to move on to another challenge. But if you find a game that makes you really think about how you want to proceed, that could be the right fit.

There are a great variety of games available to play, as I'm sure you're aware. Some games challenge you to recall information or use it in interesting ways. Other games require artistic abilities and critical thinking skills. And then there are games that may call for memorization, logical skills, or a good vocabulary. Any of these could provide a useful challenge.

Certain games are meant to be played alone, whereas others are meant to be played in groups or teams. Either format could be a good way to push yourself. However, social games are often good to play because they can require more thought. You may have to take into account the personalities of the other players and what kind of moves they're likely to make. For example, are they risk-takers or conservative? Also, there may be negotiations you have to enter in order to try to reach an advantageous position.

From playing games like chess and poker I've learned about the psychology of competition and how to find good strategies and tactics. Chess is great for pushing you to calculate all kinds of possibilities and working out the best possible moves in different situations. Poker has been useful for learning how to make certain statistical calculations quickly in order to make the best moves. Different people prefer different types of games. Find some that are interesting and challenging for you.

How to apply this habit

• Play Sudoku

• Do a Crossword Puzzle

• Play Chess

• Play Scrabble on Pogo

• Play all kinds of free games on Pogo

• Browse Wikipedia's big list of board games for ideas

Websites & Resources

• http://www.websudoku.com

• http://puzzles.usatoday.com

• http://www.chess.com

• http://www.pogo.com/games/scrabble

• http://www.pogo.com

• http://en.wikipedia.org/wiki/List_of_board_games

#12. Use Mind Training Programs

There are some mind training tools that can help you challenge and develop your mind. They tend to offer mental stimulation in different ways – doing math problems, rotating images, memorizing things, etc. It's not difficult to see how training your mind in these ways can provide a challenge and help you in improving your abilities.

There has been quite a bit of research into many mind training sites, and there isn't conclusive proof that they help you get smarter or that the skills you learn transfer over to other tasks. In any case, I still think these mind training tasks can be helpful as long as you focus on tasks that provide a challenge.

Dual-n-back is one mind training task that is especially difficult. In this task you are exposed to auditory and visual information. The goal of the person tested is to recall if the present information shown matches with what was shown several steps back. There has been mixed support for this test's ability to improve intelligence, but it certainly has not been proven that doing the training will make you smarter. Dual-n-back is a 'working memory task'. This means that it is supposed to train your ability to hold more items in your mind at one time and to make use of them as well.

Personally I view these games as fun to play around with (except for dual-n-back). They're a good way to get an idea of where your strengths and weaknesses lie, so you can train them or work on them in your daily life. For example, if you train on different sites, you may find that your memory tests very high, but your attention tests very low. In that case, you might want to take measures to improve your ability to pay attention.

How to apply this habit

- Test yourself with:
    o Cambridge Brain Sciences (free)
    o Neuro Nation (free)
    o Lumosity (free trial)
    o Dual-N-Back (free)

Websites & Resources

- http://www.cambridgebrainsciences.com
- http://www.neuronation.com
- http://www.lumosity.com

#13. Change up Your Routines

Smart people avoid being on autopilot – meaning doing things automatically without giving them any thought. When you're on autopilot you stop paying attention to new things. One way to avoid this problem is to take a new route while driving. You're more likely to notice more details because when things are new people tend to pay more attention. If you do the same tasks in the same way, you'll pay less attention and everything will blur together. You may pass the same store a hundred times and not even know what it's called. You get used to it, and drown it out in the background.

You may learn something when you take a new route – perhaps they're building a new hospital, there's an event going on, or something else. You'll expose yourself to more stimuli, and therefore more information. This helps you stay on top of what's happening in your town.

Interestingly, a study on London taxi drivers showed that they had a larger hippocampus (memory center) than people who did not drive taxis. Learning all kinds of different routes to get around town could literally change your brain if you do it enough. Of course, London is one of the biggest and most complex cities in the world, but even if your city is smaller I am sure there are plenty of new roads to learn.

The Smart Habit Guide

How to apply this habit

- Take a different route on the way to work, the store, or a friend's house
- Use your non-dominant hand for a task such as brushing your teeth or writing notes
- Go to the library or book store and pick out something to read that you normally would not
- Start a conversation with someone, even if you don't seem to have much in common

#14. Practice Observing Details in Your Environment

Intelligent people are good at noticing things other people tend to miss. They pay attention to more details. It's important not to settle for having a rough understanding of something. Think about how children will test things in many different ways. They may try to bounce an object, throw it, taste it, and squeeze it. Part of a keen observation may involve some of these sorts of tests (but probably not tasting unless it's food).

There are many kinds of observations you can make. You may notice a unique facial expression, a broken tail light on a car, or you could look more closely at something in nature. You can ask questions like *What kind of grass is that?* or *What kind of fabric is this?* And then you could take this a step further, investigating the fine details for yourself.

This is a skill that needs to be practiced for you to really become good at it. One part of the habit is close observation. Another is actively testing things to get an even better informed observation. And one more part is analyzing what you've observed and tested to come to a conclusion.

As an example, when I see something new I like to try to observe it in different ways. I like to get a good look up close, touch and feel it if I can, consider if it has a scent or some other special feature. This multi-sensory viewpoint helps me remember and understand much better.

How to apply this habit

- Pay attention to your surroundings – buildings, weather, what people are doing, etc.

- Pay attention to the reactions of people – are they happy, sad, friendly, or distracted?

- Test things to see how they work (i.e., What happens if you press a button? What happens if you do a task in a different order?)

- Pick up a flower, or anything, and look very closely – notice parts, structure, feel, smell, and other characteristics

- Pick up an everyday object you use (wallet, coin, pen), and pay attention to it closely – try to discover something about it that you never noticed before

#15. Conduct Thought Experiments

A thought experiment is when you have a hypothesis or a belief you want to test, and you proceed to think through the consequences of this hypothesis. With a thought experiment the only equipment you need is your mind and imagination.

Many times, it's impractical, unsafe, or unnecessary to test something in the real world. This is when conducting a thought experiment can be quite helpful. It could make sense to do this with tiny particles that you can't realistically work with in the real world, or with super massive objects like planets and stars. Also if you are a surgeon it could be better to play out what can happen in different scenarios in your mind, instead of actually testing things out on a living human body during a procedure.

Conducting thought experiments is great for challenging conventional beliefs, solving problems, and making predictions in areas that are difficult to test in the real world. Albert Einstein, one of the greatest minds of all time, frequently engaged in thought experiments to further his understanding of physics.

This paragraph from PBS – NOVA summarizes one of Einstein's thought experiments:

He realized that gravity and acceleration appear to be the same phenomenon. Think about what would happen if an elevator suddenly went into a free-fall. The person inside would effectively weigh nothing. Next, imagine that same person in a motionless rocket ship so far from Earth that the force of gravity is practically zero. Just like in the free-falling elevator, he would also weigh nothing. Now, put the rocket in motion. As the rocket speeds up, the passenger's weight increases. To him, it feels just as if gravity had planted his feet firmly on the floor. Einstein realized that the force of gravity is just the acceleration that you feel as you move through space-time.

Einstein was obviously an extremely intelligent and hardworking individual. He used thought experiments to further develop his understanding of time, space, gravity, and other such concepts. It's important to note that he made great discoveries at least partly as a result of his thought experiments. We could also benefit from using them in our lives.

How to apply this habit

1. Come up with an interesting question

2. Develop a hypothesis or educated guess as to what you think the answer would be

3. Think up what characters and objects you need to test your hypothesis

4. Visualize them all in your mind as vividly as you can

5. Play out a scenario that tests your hypothesis in your mind

6. If you have a problem, you may try again or choose another question to try your experiment with – not all questions can be solved through thought experiments

#16. Conduct Life Experiments

A life experiment sounds like a funny thing. I promise it's not that bad – you won't need a lab coat or a scalpel. You also don't have to engage in laboratory style precision in how you experiment with your life. In fact, you probably won't be able to. Scientists often split people up into groups, and they'll try a treatment on one group and a placebo on the other group. This allows them to see if the treatment had an effect. An example of a treatment would be testing out a new medication to see if it helps people who suffer with anxiety to reduce their symptoms. Scientists do things like choose groups randomly and they don't reveal who received the real medication and who received a placebo because this helps them to avoid bias in their results. Another thing they do is isolate variables. This means they try to create a controlled situation where the only thing that is different between the two groups is the treatment used.

In real life, we don't have the luxury of such a great level of control. There are probably many variables in your life right now that you have no control over. Maybe there is a baby crying in the other room, or a loud motorcycle is passing by outside, or telemarketers keep calling you on your phone. Even without the ability to create experiments in your life quite like a scientist may, you can still conduct a successful experiment and learn something new.

Sometimes I like to think of life experiments in a more simple way. You may think of them as a matter of trial and error. You try something new, pay attention to the feedback or the results you get, then try to make an improvement. If something works well for you, you can continue to do that unless one day it stops working. At that point, you can try experimenting again.

A lot of this book has been about learning through other sources (i.e., online sources, books, or groups in real life), but people often forget or simply don't realize that one of the best sources of knowledge is yourself. There is no one else quite like you, so just because you read that something works for other people does not guarantee it will work for you. Also, we live in a very dynamic world where things only seem to change and develop more and more rapidly. Something that worked ten years ago, or even one year ago may not work well at all today or in your exact situation. A good way to work around these issues of course, is to experiment for yourself.

How to apply this habit

1. Choose a goal

2. Make a list of the important variables, or of the things that you can change to influence your goal (i.e., if the goal is to pass a job interview, you can change your appearance, attitude, or resume)

3. If you want to know with some certainty what changes cause which effects, then change only one (or very few) variables at a time – the less variables you work with, the more certain you can be that you know how you got your results. (i.e., change your appearance to be more professional and see if you have greater success in job interviews)

4. If you're eager to get some kind of effect fast, then change multiple things that you're pretty sure are related to the outcome you want. (i.e., change your appearance to be professional, adopt a positive attitude and smile, improve your resume, *and* continue learning things relevant to your field)

5. Check what kind of results you get – seek out feedback from experts if you can, especially if you feel like you are on the wrong track

6. You may want to log your findings in a journal for future reference, then you can take a guess (i.e., hypothesis) as to what you might do to improve your results further

7. If you're happy with your results, move on to another goal and start over. If you're not happy, continue to work on the same goal with steps 2-6, but change the variables that you work on.

#17. Work Math Problems in Your Head

Knowing how to calculate basic addition, subtraction, and multiplication in your mind is a smart skill to have. It helps to make sure you don't get ripped off, and it helps to speed things up in life. If you take too long to make a mental calculation, someone else may be there to give you the answer. The issue is they may lie or they may make a miscalculation, costing you money or time. And if you think you can always use a calculator, you'd be surprised how often you don't have one when you really need it. The best calculator is in your head if you just practice using it.

Practicing holding numbers in your mind and working with them can be helpful for your working memory. This is because when doing these operations, you need to remember more in your mind as you compute something else. Practice makes you better with this sort of thing. You may feel like someone is brilliant just because they can multiply two digit numbers together, or someone can add three digit numbers or calculate a tip in seconds, but these skills are all learned. You aren't born knowing how to do this. The reason many of us are poor at some of these things is because we've never tried it or practiced it. In elementary school, they usually allow us paper and pencil to work everything out. Then in high school they allow us calculators. None of this aids our mental math abilities. We have to decide for ourselves to train in this way if we want to improve.

I have direct experience with this, as my father asked me to do mental operations in my head when I was a kid. He would write down a bunch of two digit numbers and ask me to add them without writing anything down. I thought it was impossible at first, but after a short while I started to get pretty good. By the time I got to high school I realized students relied on their calculators more and more, but I had retained the smart habit of doing basic operations in my head. This skill was more useful than I would have expected. Most of the time, even if I didn't know the exact answer to tougher problems, I could determine approximately what the answer would be.

How to apply this habit

- When you are shopping, add up the cost of items in your head and see if you were correct when you get to the checkout

- Learn some techniques for doing mental math

- Practice calculating the restaurant tip in your head – this site shows how

- Learn your multiplication tables up to 12 x 12 or 15 x 15 or even 20 x 20

- Go to a site like Neuro Nation and work math problems in your head

Websites & Resources

- http://en.wikibooks.org/wiki/Mental_Math
- http://www.wisegeek.com/contest/how-do-i-calculate-restaurant-tip-in-my-head.htm
- http://math.wikia.com/wiki/Multiplication_table_%28natural_numbers_up_to_20%29.
- http://www.neuronation.com

Socialize Your Brain

We are social animals. As humans we have evolved in a social context. Our ancestors worked together to hunt, forage for food, and ultimately build cultures and civilizations. Without communication to share information, we would be much more similar to our primate cousins – unable to make progress in our collective understanding as quickly. The most obvious way that socializing helps us learn and understand complex topics is because we share what we learn with one another. For example, if you have a friend or a mentor who is an expert in a topic, you can improve your understanding of it simply through talking about it. This is an ability we often take for granted, but we shouldn't because it is quite valuable.

Social situations can be very stimulating for us in other ways too. There are many things to pay attention to, like facial expressions, hand movements, verbal information, and whether what is said is meant literally, figuratively, or ironically. Social settings can be somewhat complex which makes them a good challenge for the mind. If you are in a group, there may be multiple people shooting ideas back and forth. You would have to gauge if you have something useful or interesting to contribute, and when it may be appropriate to do so. All of this is healthy exercise for the mind.

#18. Talk with Curious Children

Children are often very curious, and will ask interesting questions that force you to think. If you don't know many children, you might get a similar result by trying to think like a child, imagining that everything is new and amazing. Even just stepping outside you can get all sorts of questions. *What is a rainbow made of? What are the clouds made of? Why is the sky blue?* And so on.

The funny thing is that the questions usually don't stop there. Whatever you ask brings about more and more questions. This kind of curiosity is a great learning tool for a child, but it can be an opportunity to learn more for an adult as well. It's easy to get frustrated with a child and just tell him to keep quiet, or make up an answer like 'Leprechauns make rainbows and the clouds are made of pillow stuffing'. Instead, these should be taken as great opportunities to further our own understanding of the world. After all, a lot of this information is only a few mouse clicks away online.

Another reason it's a good idea to talk to curious children is that answering their questions will force you to explain what you mean very carefully. If you use a big word, you'll need to explain. If you're not clear the first time, you'll need to explain again. This can be very challenging. But if they ask something that seems too complex for them, like how a car works, you might start more simply and explain why the tires roll smoothly against the ground.

Years ago I was on a flight and a five year old girl sat down next to me. She proceeded to treat me like she had known me all of her life. She asked me many questions, like why everything looked so small outside when she looked down, why the clouds were moving by us so fast, and where I was from. Every question spawned so many more questions. The greatest challenge was to try to keep things simple but still informative for her. Nonetheless it was a fun and interesting experience, and I learned a great deal from the interaction, just as I hope she did.

I'll leave you with the fact that Einstein once said "If you can't explain it to a six year old, you don't understand it yourself."

How to apply this habit

- Encourage questions from children in your family

- Practice thinking like a naïve and curious child – keep asking 'why', for example

- Offer to give a presentation at a school or library explaining your job (or something else you're knowledgeable about) to kids – and encourage questions

- Go to r/explainlikeimfive, a forum where people explain concepts in such a way a child could understand, and see if you can offer any assistance

Websites & Resources

- http://www.reddit.com/r/explainlikeimfive

#19. Have a Stimulating Conversation with a Thought-Provoking Friend

Exchanging ideas with other smart people is a great way to push yourself further and to learn new things. Smart people are often well informed, curious about all kinds of things, and they tend to have a lot of ideas on their mind. You can easily learn all sorts of things in a conversation with such a person.

If you make errors in your thinking or in your understanding of something, you're more likely to be corrected in smart company. At the very least, you're likely to hear about new perspectives on an issue that you may not have considered in the past. Smarter people tend to consider multiple perspectives instead of automatically choosing one side.

Intelligent people are often well aware of many fields or domains, and the best way to approach different problems. You may find a faster or better way of doing something simply by having a casual conversation with a smart person.

I'm certain that many of my conversations with smart and curious people have shaped my understanding of many domains and of the world. These interactions have influenced my mind and my thinking. One great example of how much others have made an impact on me is in the habits I've discussed here. Most if not all of the habits in this book are ones I've seen people use that I considered quite smart.

How to apply this habit in your life

- Read a newspaper or scientific magazine article and discuss it with a well-educated friend

- If you're a student, stay after class and ask the teacher questions – they don't necessarily have to be limited to the topic of the day

- Make conversation with professionals or people who work in a different field than you and see if you can learn something new

#20. Teach or Show Someone How to Perform a Task

You might think you know a topic really well, but a good test of how well you know something is to teach it. You have to really know it to teach it. Think about it, someone who is teaching or showing someone else how to do a task is expected to have mastered the topic. If a student asks a basic question, or even a somewhat in depth question, the teacher is usually expected to know the answer or to at least have a good idea as to how to think through the topic to arrive at the right answer.

To teach, you have to think from the perspective of someone who knows just the basics, or perhaps even less. It's a challenge. It's not enough to know the correct answer to a problem, but you have to be able to explain it in a way that makes sense to someone with little understanding of the topic. As easy as it may sound to explain something you already know how to do, experts can actually have a difficult time with this.

At times, students ask tough questions that can make you think deeper about a topic. A teacher may be familiar with a topic deeply, but still be unable to answer some questions. When you teach or explain something to another person, you're often forced to realize your own limited understanding of a topic.

Teaching can help you identify those gaps so you know what you should work on.

How to apply this habit in your life

- When you see a fellow student or worker stuck on a problem you know how to handle, volunteer to help

- Volunteer to tutor at a local school or at an adult learning center – there are many people who could use help learning

- If you're good at math or other tough topics, go to a forum like Mathgoodies or Able2Know to help kids on a problem

Websites & Resources

- http://www.mathgoodies.com/
- https://able2know.org/forums

#21. Practice Thinking Clearly

It's a good idea to take a pause instead of saying the first thing that comes to mind. This will allow you the time to refine your ideas and thoughts into simple, clear, direct messages that can be easily understood. The purpose of communication is of course to get thoughts across clearly.

We often value quick thinkers who can come up with a good answer off the top of their heads, but the best and most direct answers tend to come with some thought behind them. You have to consider who the audience is. What do they know and what do they expect to hear? If you are communicating about a sensitive issue, it's also important to take people's feelings into account.

Even if you intuitively know what you want to say right away, it takes a few seconds to know exactly the words you should use to be clear to your audience. Sometimes we understand something very well, but communication can be a form of teaching, and teaching something to another person can involve extra considerations. Perhaps something you understand easily or intuitively is actually a challenge for other people. That is something you would have to take into account.

It's more challenging to come up with a concise and clear message than it is to say the first thing that comes to mind – making the extra effort can be a good exercise for your mind. To do this, you need to take a moment to decide the best way to phrase statements, what your objectives are, and what your goals are in your communication with someone. If you always said what you thought immediately, you may find yourself making statements that aren't well supported, taking longer to explain something simple, or possibly even offending people because you didn't take their perspective into account.

How to apply this habit

- Pause before you speak and think through what you want to say

- Practice organizing your thoughts before you choose a side on an issue

- Try writing out your thoughts – this is a good way to analyze your thinking and make sure it is coherent, structured, and useful to other people

- If you're unable to think up a good coherent answer within a minute, ask for extra time to do some research and get your thoughts in order

#22. Practice Speaking Clearly

It's important to articulate your words, and to avoid speaking too fast. Remember, the purpose of communication is to get ideas across clearly. When you go much faster than the usual speeds, you will lose people – including their understanding, and possibly their interest. Sometimes I find myself getting lost when people speak too fast. I need a bit of time to process the ideas. And trust me, I'm not alone in this. It's important to make sure people can understand what you say and mean when you communicate.

Make an effort to state your words clearly and accurately. Many words sound similar but mean different things. Look them up if you're not sure. It can be silly and confusing to use the wrong word with a completely different meaning than the one you intended. As an example, you wouldn't 'take her for granite', but you might 'take her for granted' (even though you shouldn't). They sound similar, but the first statement doesn't make sense while the second one does.

Smart people tend to work on their communication skills. They make an effort to understand exactly what people mean. They also make an effort to be properly understood. A simple way to be better understood is to speak more clearly and to enunciate words as the dictionary suggests. One way to get yourself moving in the right direction is to spend more time with people who prioritize speaking clearly and well. You could learn something just by listening.

How to apply this habit

- If people tell you that you talk too fast, make a conscious effort to slow down – and tell your friends to point out when you speak too fast for them

- Look up words on Merriam-Webster online if you aren't sure how to enunciate them – there is a 'speaker' symbol next to the word you search that can be pressed to play a recording of the word

- Practice saying words aloud that have given you any trouble, and ask an educated friend if you are saying the word correctly

Websites & Resources

- http://www.merriam-webster.com/dictionary

Practice Your Memory

Memory is a cornerstone to developing a smarter mind. For everything you learn and do, you must remember your experiences in order to really make sense of them and progress in your understanding. No one can remember everything, but there are ways you can improve your ability to recall specific things.

In today's society our memories are becoming more externalized. This means we rely on computers, smartphones, and other devices or notebooks to store important information for us. Therefore, we're less likely to practice our memories because all of the information we need is readily available. Although this can be a very convenient setup, it's important that we exercise our memories if we want to keep them sharp and reliable.

It's easy to think that you're born with the memory you have, but it is actually something that can be trained to a great degree. One interesting case was with Joshua Foer, author of "Moonwalking with Einstein", who was able to graduate his memory from seemingly ordinary to winning the USA Memory Championship. He accomplished this by training his memory specifically for what was tested in the Championship. But this section of the book focuses more on practical memory advice for everyday use. In any case, the point is that your memory itself can be improved (and quite drastically) if you work on it.

#23. Use the Peg System to Remember Lists in Order

The peg system involves learning ten pegs. Think of pegs as hooks where you can hang new information so that you can more easily remember new things. This system works well for learning a list of ten items or less in order. As an example, you can learn this common rhyming peg:

- 1 is a gun
- 2 is a shoe
- 3 is a tree
- 4 is a door
- 5 is a hive
- 6 is bricks
- 7 is heaven
- 8 is weight
- 9 is wine
- 10 is a hen

This can take a minute or so to memorize. When you've learned this list, you can use these items as pegs or hooks to help you remember a new list.

For example, a list of groceries and miscellaneous items may include:

1. Bananas
2. Milk
3. Ketchup
4. Bacon
5. Dish soap
6. Bread
7. Punch
8. Cheese
9. Bagels
10. A Notebook

Now, the task is to visualize the items you want to remember along with your peg system. For example:

- Visualize:
    - A gun that fires off a banana into the air
    - You go to put on your shoes, but they're filled with milk
    - Outside, instead of the tree you usually see, this time it has ketchup bottles growing on it
    - A door made of bacon
    - A bee hive with soap suds oozing out of it
    - A house made of brick. All of a sudden the bricks turn to bread and the house crumbles down

o You've made it to heaven, and everyone is drinking punch, inviting you to join

o A scale at the grocery store. Someone puts a piece of cheese so large on the scale that it breaks

o A wine glass. Instead of wine, there is a bagel in your glass

o A hen. You throw some food to it but it lands on a notebook. The hen pecks away at the food and the pages on the notebook

This is a mnemonic trick that is fairly easy to learn and implement. The pegs can be learned in a matter of a minute or two, so you can get started memorizing lists pretty quickly. The trick to the system is visualizing as vividly as you can. It helps to think of things that are more shocking or bizarre to really solidify them in your memory.

It's pretty common to be in a situation where you want to remember several items. You may want to remember grocery items, a to-do list, or perhaps a list of things you need to remember for school. There are plenty of opportunities where you may want to use memory pegs to aid your memory. Of course, most of us have something to write with, but sometimes we forget that or we are caught in a situation where we didn't expect to need to write anything down. Rather than get frustrated, it can be helpful to use the peg system to remember what you need to know. A caveat is that you should take a moment to visualize how what you want to remember links to your pegs. If you rush the process, you may not remember.

How to apply this habit

- Use the peg system to:
    - remember a grocery list in order
    - remember the first ten presidents in order
    - remember your to-do list in order

#24. Memorize Numbers

With our external memories in the form of computers, planners, and smart phones, hardly anyone seems to remember many numbers anymore. If you need an address or a phone number, it's easier to just look it up most of the time. In any case, it can be a very useful skill to practice remembering numbers. Most people today know very few phone numbers – they're unlikely to even know the numbers of family members or close friends.

A good exercise to try is learning numbers and to practice recalling them. If the exercise seems silly and pointless, keep in mind that one day you might really need a phone number of someone close to you, and you may not have your smartphone with you in an emergency. This is something that really doesn't take very long to do, and it could really be useful.

I'm an example of how a memory for numbers can decline when it's rarely used. When I was a child I liked learning numbers. I still remember my grandfather's old phone number very clearly. He hasn't lived in the location of that phone for about 20 years. However, when it comes to today, there are close friends and family whose numbers I would struggle to remember. To be honest, no matter how much I struggle, I still wouldn't recall some of them. I've gotten used to my smartphone doing all of the work like many people have. Nonetheless, it's a good challenge for your mind to practice remembering numbers once in a while.

How to apply this habit

- Practice remembering:
  - Phone numbers of friends and relatives
  - Your social security or government issued identification number
  - The miles on your car's odometer and test yourself before you start the car again
  - Your license plate number
  - Your credit card number if you want a bit of an extra challenge

#25. Remember Your Day

In order to retain your memories over the long term, it really helps to practice remembering them day by day. If you ever find yourself having difficulty remembering something you did, or what happened at an event you attended, simply recalling your life periodically can help strengthen your memories. Every time you concentrate on remembering something that happened, you recreate that memory in your mind and you make it stronger.

This is a good analytic task as well being a memory task. You may realize something when you play back your memories that you didn't catch the first time around. For example, you might recall that a friend called you and you promised to get back to her, but you never did. There are all kinds of details you may notice if you play back your memories.

Since I've started playing back my day at night, I find that my memory is improving. Sometimes I challenge myself to remember specific details like what a friend of mine was wearing or what my work tasks were for the day or what exactly was said in a conversation. Doing this has helped me improve my attention and my ability to remember things.

How to apply this habit

- Practice remembering everything you did for the day in order

- To trigger memories, you can ask yourself questions such as:

    o What did you do at school or work?

    o What conversations did you have?

    o What did you eat?

    o What clothing did you or your coworkers wear?

    o Did anything unusual happen?

#26. If You Forget Something, Retrace Your Steps

Everyone forgets what they were doing occasionally. It's important to know what to do when that happens. Don't get frustrated, instead just retrace your steps.

First, try to retrace your steps mentally. By doing this, you force your mind to work extra hard, thinking through everything you just did. If you forget what you were going to say, you can try to retrace what just happened in the conversation. What were you saying? What was the other person saying? What is your general topic? Has anything happened recently that relates to these topics, that perhaps you wanted to mention?

If that doesn't work, you can always retrace your steps physically, which is likely to reactivate what you wanted to do because you'll see the same stimuli. Of course, this only works for certain kinds of forgetting. If you forget your place in a conversation, it may not make much sense to retrace your steps physically, especially if you were sitting still. But if you walked into a room and forgot what you came for, you can always return to the first room you were in. Perhaps you were doing something that made you think you needed to go to the other room to find an item.

It doesn't always work, but putting in the effort to remember something can help sharpen your memory.

How to apply this habit in your life

- Retrace your steps mentally when you forget something
  - o Think about what you were saying
  - o Think about what your conversation partner was saying
  - o Recall what the general topic was
  - o Recall if anything interesting happened recently that you wanted to talk about
- Retrace your steps physically if retracing them mentally didn't work for you
  - o Go back to the room you started in
  - o Get into the same position and touch the same items or look at the same items that triggered you to leave the room

#27. Rearrange Your Items

Assuming all of your items are always in the same place doesn't challenge your mind. A good exercise is to move around everyday items that you use. When you get used to assuming everything is in the same place, you have no reason to use your memory. It's a good idea to put extra challenges on your memory to keep it strong. If we don't do this, our ability to remember can get worse over time.

Moving things around trains you to pay attention to change, which aids your memory. You learn to not assume that everything is always in the same place. You'll begin to pay attention when you move an item. This exercise may seem somewhat trivial, but it's an easy way to challenge yourself to remember.

I have a few important items that I tend to disperse randomly throughout the house. They're my shoes, coat, wallet, phone, and keys. This isn't completely intentional, it often just happens because I don't have a routine of putting all of my things in one place. I used to spend time looking through different rooms in the morning for all of my belongings, but now I take a moment and think where I left everything. Sometimes I still forget, but by practicing this my recall has gotten to the point where I often remember where I left everything.

How to apply this habit

- In the shower, move around your soap, shampoo, and conditioner (or other items) – Before your next shower, try to recall where you left everything

- Take something small (and not easily confused with other items) like a refrigerator magnet and put it in a new hiding spot every few days – your task is to remember where you hid it

- Put some important items (i.e., wallet, phone) in different places throughout the house and try to recall where you left them the next day

#28. Push Yourself to Remember

When asked a question, sometimes it feels easier to say that you don't know or you don't remember. But perhaps you do know, you just haven't pushed yourself hard enough to remember. If the solution doesn't come to you automatically, think a bit further. Is the question or topic something you've worked with in the past? Is it something you've done? What have you done or observed in the past in regards to the topic?

When you do a mental search for the answer, you may find that you know more than you think. Perhaps you can combine logic and memory. You may remember that there are three things you need to do to complete a task, but you may not be sure of the order that they need to be done. However, if you think through logically, you may realize that the process only works out successfully if you do it in a specific order. By going through these steps you put your mind through a challenge that strengthens it. If you keep doing this, your memory and mental abilities will improve.

One of the reasons I mention this smart habit is because I used to have the bad habit of saying "I don't know" too fast, rather than doing a mental search for the memories I needed to solve the problem. I now realize that saying "I don't know" is not only annoying when said too often, but if I take a moment to think, sometimes I actually do know the answer. At least if I don't know the full answer, it often turns out that I knew more than I gave myself credit for.

How to apply this habit

- Pausing before you speak (as in Habit #21) is a good idea here too, so you allow yourself a moment to reflect on your memories and come up with an answer

- Ask a friend or significant other to remind you to think if you say "I don't know" or "I don't remember" too fast to a question (especially if he/she is aware that you should know the answer)

- Use all of your senses to help you remember (i.e., were there any sounds or smells related to your memory?)

#29. Associate Your Experiences with Prior Memories

This habit is actually very simple, but I've found it can help to bring back memories that seemed temporarily lost. All you do is pick any object or even a situation or event, but objects are simpler. As an example, you may pick a tree in your backyard. The task then is to think back to any memories you can recall with that tree. The more unusual the object is, the more likely you'll come up with vivid memories more easily, assuming you had prior memories with the object.

What you would do in this case is recall as vividly as you can all of your memories with, near, or involving that tree in the backyard. Did you climb the tree as a child? Did you prune it or hire someone to prune it? Did you plant the tree or buy it? Can you recall any specific animals or birds that have lived in or near that tree? You get the idea. You would think about everything you possibly can related to your chosen object or event.

The point of this exercise is that you may surprise yourself at the vividness of memories you can recall if you simply use your immediate environment as a starting point to remember. You can use this habit in different ways. For example, if you go outside at night and gaze at the stars, try to remember back to different times in your life you did that same thing. If you arrive late to work, think back to other times this happened.

The more you practice your memory the better it becomes. It may seem very difficult at first to think up specific details from the past, but with practice you can become better. Often, there are memories hidden within us, but we have to search to find them. Through the years they've become hidden behind layers of new memories. The good news is you can learn to uncover them by practicing this habit.

How to apply this habit

- Take something in your immediate environment and think back to other memories you've had with that object – You can also do this with events or experiences

- When you see a friend or acquaintance you haven't seen in several days or longer, think back to the last conversation you had, or the last thing you both did together (This can be a good social habit too.)

- You can even take a word you see in a book, and think back to what the word has meant to you – when did you learn the meaning and in what contexts have you seen the word?

Useful Life Habits

Really, all of the habits in this book should hopefully be useful to you in some way. This section will include more such habits that you can implement in your everyday life. They are simple to use, they're effective, and they can help you further develop your intellectual abilities.

#30. Ask for Help When You Need it

Running into a difficult challenge happens to everyone. Just because you don't know how to do something doesn't mean you'll never figure it out. When this happens, it's a good idea to find someone who knows more about the topic and who can help you learn. You may be uncomfortable seeking help, but if you aren't making any progress or if you're falling behind on something important that you want or need to learn, sometimes there is no better option. The good thing is there is usually someone more than willing to help if you look around.

It's common to need help at some point, and it really makes a difference to get that help instead of trying to force yourself over and over to come up with a solution. Especially if you are getting no results by doing this. If you are studying or learning a difficult topic, you may be surprised at just how many people need tutors and extra help.

As an example, I made a mistake when I was a freshman in high school. Algebra was the hardest thing in the world for me, but I refused to get help. I'd spend frustrating hours studying at night, still with a poor understanding. Eventually after months of hanging on by a thread, I decided to get help. Luckily, my teacher offered to tutor me in the mornings. I went from a frustrated C/D student with horrible understanding, to a comfortable A-/ B+ student with a very good understanding after two months of tutoring. I don't think I could have gotten caught up without the extra help. An important thing I want to note is that to this day I consider myself pretty strong in algebra. I had to work so hard to learn it (with the help of a great teacher) that even after years of not using it I can still recall the main principles.

How to apply this habit

If you feel lost:

- Ask a teacher, mentor, a friend, or someone knowledgeable for help

- Seek out a study group, or start one of your own

- Find a helpful forum online where you can ask questions by Googling [Problem topic area + "forum"]

#31. Form Analogies

Analogies are great for explaining concepts to other people, and also helpful for solidifying your own understanding of a topic. As you know, an analogy usually compares what you're trying to learn with something else that you already know. It's like a bridge that builds a path toward a better understanding. This is one of the fastest ways you can form new connections and begin to clearly understand a topic.

With an analogy, something that is complex can be made simple and easy to understand – this is very powerful. A concept that is shapeless and confusing can suddenly take shape and make perfect sense with the right analogy. Analogies are about taking what is commonly known and bringing clarity to a topic that you don't quite understand yet. They are great both for teaching and learning new concepts and ideas.

As an example, in the movie "Forrest Gump", Forrest says "Life is like a box of chocolates. You never know what you're going to get." This is actually a pretty good example of an analogy, because Forrest uses something concrete and easily understood, a box of chocolates, to explain something more abstract and not always easily understood, life. Of course, life is much more complex than just a box of chocolates. But the point of an analogy isn't to perfectly explain something complex, it's to help foster understanding in a practical way.

How to apply this habit

- Come up with some analogies that apply in your day to day life – what is a good analogy for what you do at work? What is a good analogy for a hobby that you invest a lot of time into? Perhaps you can use these analogies to quickly explain what you do to others

- Compare concepts that you don't fully understand with other systems that you're more familiar with

- Learn broadly about how different systems work so you have more analogies in mind to quickly learn new things (i.e., mechanics, anatomy and physiology, evolution, etc.)

#32. Write Down Your Thoughts (or Record Them)

Getting your thoughts down into words on paper makes you break them down and forces you to clarify exactly what you think, and why you think it. It's a challenge. When writing, it's usually a good idea to put down reasons why you feel or think the way you do. This causes you to actively think about the situation, consider alternative viewpoints, and evaluate specifically how you came to your conclusions.

Writing is a good exercise for your memory, because you'll often want to think back on experiences you've had that support your argument or your thoughts on something. The more events you can recall from memory that support a point, the more likely you are to feel strongly that you have good reason to believe what you do. If you find weak support in your memories, you may decide it's better to question your thinking, and perhaps you've been too quick to take a position on an issue.

Another useful part about writing is that by maintaining a record of your thoughts, you can always look back on them later. In the future you'll be able to look back on your thoughts and evaluate if you've learned something new that invalidates your old thoughts. Or perhaps you will have learned something new that further supports what you used to think. Another possibility is that you've moved on and found issues that are of greater importance than the ones you used to worry about.

I've kept logs occasionally of some of my thoughts throughout my life. It's interesting to look back and see what kinds of things were important to me at different points in life. Logging my thoughts and experiences has helped me to better evaluate where I've been and where I want to be in the future.

How to apply this habit

- Record your progress on an important goal in your life

- Record a great learning experience that you had

- Write about a mistake you made and what you learned from it

- Write down your thoughts on a book you read and what you learned

- As you record your thoughts, look for supporting memories or facts for why you hold your conclusions and write them down as well

#33. Organize Your Notes

If you have notes (or files of them) for work that are important for you to know and understand, then organizing them physically can also help you organize them mentally. You may feel comfortable having all of your notes available to you, but this alone isn't enough for them to be useful. To really understand them, the notes have to be organized. You'll probably want to have them neatly filed or in a notebook or binder. But beyond that, the information needs to be arranged in a way that makes it more likely for you to understand and remember. Intelligence isn't just about knowing more facts. It's also about understanding how things connect, how they're organized, and how they work.

If you have trouble understanding something, you might make a mind map, an outline, a flow chart, or a Venn diagram to further break it down into simple steps that really make sense. (If you're not familiar with these, informative links are provided at the end of this section.) You may even create a dictionary of terms for yourself if you find that certain concepts are giving you a lot of problems with comprehending your notes.

When I have trouble understanding a field or a topic, I like to mind map it out to see how everything interrelates and interconnects. Of course, your preference for organizing your notes really depends on your expertise level, how your mind works, and your area of study. Perhaps for your notes, a flow chart or a Venn diagram makes more sense than a mind map. This is something you need to consider.

How to apply this habit

- Use a notebook, Evernote, or another program, to organize files and delete or put into a junk folder items that are no longer important

- Make an outline

- Make a mind map

- Make a flow chart

- Make a Venn diagram

- Create a dictionary of terms (where you define all important concepts)

Websites & Resources

- https://evernote.com/download

- http://en.wikipedia.org/wiki/Mind_map

- http://en.wikipedia.org/wiki/Flowchart

- http://en.wikipedia.org/wiki/Venn_diagram

#34. Define Your Top Goal for the Day

Smart people get things done, and I find this to be one of the simplest and most useful habits to help focus and get things done. Sure, you can write down your #2 and #3 goals, but usually my #1 goal dictates the whole tone of a day. My #2 and #3 and so forth goals will often come about naturally as things I need to do to support my #1 goal for the day.

A clear directed focus is an important part of being smart. A great way to do that is to know exactly what you want to accomplish the next day, especially the biggest priority. Intelligent people avoid wasting time in the morning. They already know beforehand what the most important thing they need to do is. It's easy to burn up time doing things that are not so important when we don't have some kind of plan. This is why it's important to at least know your top goal for the day every day. It's a good idea either to make a note of this the night before, or at least to get up early in the morning to make sure you know your top priority.

This smart habit comes from personal experience. When I don't have my goal for the day clearly laid out, I find that I may not get started on anything important until later in the day. If I don't have a plan, the first few hours of my day will tend to go toward things that may be easier, but not especially important. I make sure to always follow this habit now, because I know it really helps.

How to apply this habit

- Before you go to bed, get a notecard and write down your #1 priority for the next day that you absolutely want to accomplish – consider an item that if you were to accomplish it, would bring you closer to meeting your biggest goals

- If you think of a few tasks that support that goal, you can write those down as well

- Make sure to put 100% of your focus on your top priority until you are finished

#35. Think Ahead and Have Backup Plans

Many of us might like to plan something and then stick to that plan. Having a plan often helps as opposed to having no idea how you want to do something. However, plans can change, sometimes in ways you didn't expect. Not only this, but so many things happen in the course of the day that it's not realistic to try to plan ahead for absolutely everything.

As a result of plans changing frequently, and being unable to plan for everything, it's a smart habit to regularly be thinking ahead. This is a good way to avoid auto-piloting and keeping your mind active. If you're driving, you may think "What's next?" *First I'm dropping off the kids at daycare. Then I'm going to stop at the coffee shop for breakfast. Then I'll going to work but I have to take a different street because the one I usually take is shut off.* As simple as this all seems, if you're not thinking ahead it's easy to waste time or make a costly mistake.

Thinking about what's next is a very useful habit. It can involve memory, as in the example above the driver remembers that there is construction and he should take a different way to work. It obviously involves planning skills, and you may have to predict if you do one action, what will happen next. You may evaluate if there are better alternatives. This can involve questioning and analyzing possibilities. This is a useful habit because you can save time and avoid problems.

How to apply this habit

- When driving, ask yourself how you can best get to your destination efficiently

- When doing your work, ask yourself what you need to do after you finish your current project

- For important events, try to come up with at least one backup plan that you can implement if everything doesn't work out exactly as you expected

#36. Make Learning Fun, Interesting, and Relevant

Sometimes you have to learn something because it's important for school, work, or some other important need, and you don't have much of a choice. In that case, you need to find a way to make it fun and interesting. Smart people know how to learn even when they're not in the mood. Usually, they will be happy to learn because smart people tend to be quite curious, but no one is always in the mood to learn everything.

It's important to do this because if your brain interprets what you're learning as dry and boring, then you're going to have to repeat the material to yourself over and over just to learn it because your brain is telling you 'this doesn't really matter'. When you find a way to make learning fun, engaging, and relevant to your life, it will come much easier. You'll begin to absorb the material in a way you otherwise wouldn't.

One thing I'll do is look hard to determine a way that what I'm learning is relevant to me personally, or figuring out a scenario when I might need to use it. This can be a stretch, especially for more abstract topics or topics that involve past time periods. One thing that keeps me going is that I don't like to be seen as ignorant. This can only take me so far though. If the pressure is high to learn something I feel is boring, I may try to turn learning the material into a fun challenge of some kind.

How to apply this habit

- Practice making up funny stories out of what you're learning

- Practice finding personal relevancy in what you learn

- Practice dramatizing what you learn, as if it were a Hollywood movie

- For stories or history, pretend that you are the main character – this helps make it matter and become emotionally vivid

#37. Apply What You Read or Learn

You should realize that the best way to truly learn something is to try it for yourself. It's important to make sure that when a topic is important to you that you don't get too hung up on reading or analyzing endlessly. Reading and analyzing are good ways of learning and developing your thinking, but at some point the best thing you can do is put what you know to use.

It's common for people to worry about making a mistake, and this is a real possibility in anything we do. When the possible mistakes are more costly, perhaps it's a good idea to read more and analyze more. But when the possible mistakes are not likely to cost you much, it's better to read less, analyze less, and do something instead. You can learn a lot from putting to use what you've learned in books and through thinking and planning. Often times things won't go like you planned, or you'll make mistakes you didn't expect to make. And the best thing you can do is learn from those mistakes.

If you've been reading about gardening for a while, you might want to take the plunge and buy some seeds or small plants and get them in the ground already. If you've been reading about swimming technique but you don't know how to swim, you could be better off signing up for lessons from a good instructor. Also, if you've visited art museums to get a good idea of how to make a painting, you might want to pick up a brush already and start somewhere.

The problem we have sometimes is that we get stuck in a rut of reading and analyzing instead of acting and doing. Feel free to read and analyze, just make an effort to catch yourself when all you're doing is building up fear that you'll make a mistake instead of taking the plunge and seeing what you can actually do.

How to apply this habit

- While reading or learning something new, ask yourself frequently how the material applies to your life and how you can adapt the information for your specific needs

- If you get stuck in a rut of analyzing the same possibilities over and over, or if you find yourself worrying more about what can go wrong than about how to make progress, you should consider pushing through and taking action – Of course, analysis makes sense when the risks are too high to jump in

- If you have a teacher that doesn't clearly state the practical use of what they teach, then go ahead and ask

Putting Smart Habits into Action

Remember that smart habits are different than other kinds of habits. If you find that you routinely and easily implement a habit, change your focus to something else. Instead of doing one thing over and over, keep your mind sharp by working on different smart habits. I will usually only focus on a few at a time. Through using some of them frequently, like asking questions (Habit # 6) and doing math problems in my head (Habit #17), they've become somewhat automatic. They're good to do, but I don't need to think about them or plan to use them. Instead, I tend to focus on habits that give me more of a challenge and that I might not do automatically, like pushing myself to remember (Habit #28) or thinking ahead (Habit #35).

Plan - Do - Check - Act
(as shown on the book cover)

This system for using habits is fairly straightforward. It's not essential that you use it, but it's a helpful way to think about habits and to implement them in your life. **First, plan out which habits you want to use.** Maybe you only want to focus on one section, like "Challenge Yourself and Try New Things" or perhaps you want to try them all. Choose the ones that are important for your goals. **Second, do the habits.** Try them out and see how it goes. **Third, check on your progress.** Is there anything you can do to use the habits better? Do you need more practice or is there a better habit that might meet your needs? **Last, you should act.** This means you take action, applying the habits important for your goals. If you're only able to do one habit at a time, that is fine. If you want to try three or four, you can do that as well. Again, when you master a habit, I recommend looking for a new smart habit to work on. This way, you'll always be challenged.

From Here, Where Do You Go?

If Plan – Do – Check – Act is too much to worry about, then just work on your smart habits as you have time. The important part is to make sure you are challenging your mind. The common denominator in all of the habits in this book is that they are meant to challenge you in some way. You don't want to get frustrated with too much challenge, and you don't want to do things that are too easy for you. It's important to find the right balance. Those are the best smart habits. You may even discover some of your own smart habits that you can use, and that's great too.

I've observed these habits in some of the smartest people I've known, and some I've discovered for myself. The ones I discovered myself were often by finding that I used bad habits that weren't working for me or someone pointed out that I had a bad habit. I don't claim to be perfect and always follow every habit listed. It's an ongoing effort, but I believe they are very worthwhile and I will continue to make efforts to implement them in my life. The best part of course is that these are habits anyone can get started with right away.

I'd like to add one last piece of advice before I leave you to get started. As I've pointed out, I learned about many smart habits through observation. If there was a time I realized I had done something foolish, I would simply stop and ask myself what I could have done better. If I noticed that someone I considered smart had a specific habit that got them results, I paid attention to that. Sometimes I would even ask what they were thinking or how they came to a solution to a problem. You may be surprised at what you can learn simply through observation and asking questions.

Through my observations and questions, I've only come to believe more strongly that what separates the very smart from everyone else is that they've learned what kind of habits get the best results. They tend to be the habits that challenge the mind and that involve learning and striving to understand more and more. After identifying those habits, they've committed themselves to taking action and using them regularly. The habits you need to get started are in this book. To improve your abilities and get results in your life you will have to put them into action.

Thank You

Thank you for taking the time to read *The Smart Habit Guide*. I hope that you found the information useful. Just remember that a key part of the learning process is putting what you read into practice.

Before you go, I want to invite you to pick up your free copy of *Step Up Your Learning: Free Tools to Learn Almost Anything*. All you have to do is type this link into your browser:

http://bit.ly/Robledo

Also, if you have any questions, comments, or feedback about this book, you can send me a message and I'll get back to you as soon as possible. Please put the title of the book you are commenting on in the subject line. My email address is:

ic.robledo@mentalmax.net

Did You Learn Something New?

If you found value in this book, please review it on Amazon so I can stay focused on writing more great books. Even a short one or two sentences would be helpful.

To go directly to the review page, you may type this into your web browser:

http://hyperurl.co/l6x1z9

An Invitation to the "Master Your Mind" Community (on Facebook)

I founded a community where we can share advice or tips on our journey to mastering the mind. Whether you want to be a better learner, improve your creativity, get focused, or work on other such goals, this will be a place to find helpful information and a supportive network. I hope you join us and commit to taking your mind to a higher level.

To go directly to the page to join the community, you may type this into your web browser:

http://hyperurl.co/xvbpfc

More Books by I. C. Robledo

The Secret Principles of Genius

The Intellectual Toolkit of Geniuses

55 Smart Apps to Level Up Your Brain

No One Ever Taught Me How to Learn

Ready, Set, Change

Idea Hacks

To see the full list of authored books, visit:

www.Amazon.com/author/icrobledo

Appendix: List of Websites & Resources

Note: To click on the websites, go to the following site: **https://goo.gl/a1Udfi**

Learn Something Every Day

http://theweek.com

http://www.bbc.com

http://www.economist.com

http://en.wikipedia.org/wiki/special:random

http://www.world-english.org/stories.htm

http://www.freebooks.com

http://www.openculture.com/free_ebooks

http://www.openculture.com/free_textbooks

http://video.nationalgeographic.com/

http://www.ted.com/

http://www.reddit.com/r/Documentaries/

http://video.pbs.org/program/nova/

http://www.google.com/videohp?hl=en

https://www.youtube.com/

http://www.openculture.com/freemoviesonline

http://www.apple.com/itunes/download

http://www.merriam-webster.com/word-of-the-day

http://www.amazon.com/dp/B003IS768K

https://www.duolingo.com/

http://www.reddit.com/r/languagelearning/

http://www.openculture.com/freelanguagelessons

http://lifehacker.com/5903288/i-learned-to-speak-four-languages-in-a-few-years-heres-how

http://fourhourworkweek.com/2014/03/21/how-to-learn-a-foreign-language-2

https://www.quora.com

http://www.reddit.com

http://stackexchange.com

http://www.insectidentification.org/identifying.asp

http://www.arborday.org/trees/whatTree

http://animals.nationalgeographic.com/animals/birding/backyard-bird-identifier

https://www.khanacademy.org

http://www.oeconsortium.org/courses

http://ocw.mit.edu/index.htm

https://www.coursera.org

https://www.edx.org

http://www.openculture.com/free_certificate_courses

http://www.openculture.com/freeonlinecourses

http://www.reddit.com/r/answers

http://www.reddit.com/r/askscience

http://www.reddit.com/r/changemyview

http://www.reddit.com/r/IWantToLearn

https://www.quora.com

http://stackexchange.com

http://www.meetup.com

Challenge Yourself and Try New Things

http://www.websudoku.com

http://puzzles.usatoday.com

http://www.chess.com

http://www.pogo.com/games/scrabble

http://www.pogo.com

http://en.wikipedia.org/wiki/List_of_board_games

http://www.cambridgebrainsciences.com

http://www.neuronation.com

http://www.lumosity.com

http://en.wikibooks.org/wiki/Mental_Math

http://www.wisegeek.com/contest/how-do-i-calculate-restaurant-tip-in-my-head.htm

http://math.wikia.com/wiki/Multiplication_table_%28natural_numbers_up_to_20%29

http://www.neuronation.com

Socialize Your Brain
http://www.reddit.com/r/explainlikeimfive

http://www.mathgoodies.com/

https://able2know.org/forums

http://www.merriam-webster.com/dictionary

Useful Life Habits
https://evernote.com/download

http://en.wikipedia.org/wiki/Mind_map

http://en.wikipedia.org/wiki/Flowchart

http://en.wikipedia.org/wiki/Venn_diagram

Printed in Great Britain
by Amazon